THE WHOLE MARIE

WINNER OF THE SAWTOOTH POETRY PRIZE 2008

C.D. WRIGHT, judge

THE WHOLE MARIE

BARBARA MALOUTAS

BOISE STATE UNIVERSITY • BOISE • IDAHO • 2009

Ahsahta Press, Boise State University
Boise, Idaho 83725
http://ahsahtapress.boisestate.edu
http://ahsahtapress.boisestate.edu/books/maloutas/maloutas.htm

Printed in the United States of America
Cover design by Quemadura
Book design by Janet Holmes
First printing January 2009
ISBN-13: 978-1-934103-04-3

Library of Congress Cataloging-in-Publication Data

Maloutas, Barbara.
The whole Marie / Barbara Maloutas.
p. cm.
Poems.
ISBN-13: 978-1-934103-04-3 (pbk. : alk. paper)
ISBN-10: 1-934103-04-7 (pbk. : alk. paper)
I. Title.

PS3613.A47W46 2009
811'.6--DC22

2008041104

ACKNOWLEDGMENTS

Sections of "Abiding Delacroix" ("Paris October 12," "Tuesday October 22," "last Tuesday," "Paris Tuesday April 15," "Monday January 12," "same day," "Sunday January 25," "Saturday April 10," "Tuesday April 20," and "Saturday May 15 during the day") and "hunting dogs" appeared in *bird dog*. Sections 8 and 9 of "on Porto" appeared online in *DIAGRAM*. Sections of "tableaux vivant" ("direction 1," "direction 2," "direction 6," and "direction 8") appeared online in *dusie*. "direction 5" from "tableaux vivant" appeared online in *FreeVerse*. "when I read" appeared in *Greatcoat*. Sections 1–6 of "on Porto" appeared in *OR*. "possessive pronomial adjective" and "bookkeepers" appeared online in *Segue*. "Cavafy," "Pieces," "Orthodoxy," "Bratsera," and "Oracle" appeared as an online chapbook in *Segue* along with an essay on writing the series. "Trap" appeared in *Tarpaulin Sky's Print Issue 1*.

CONTENTS

TERRIBLE/GEOGRAPHY

1:11, ALMOST

this learning to tell time
his learning to tell time
is learning to tell time
learning to tell time
learning to tell   me
is learning to tell   me
his learning to tell   me
this learning to tell   me
this learning to tell i'm
his learning to tell i'm
is learning to tell i'm
learning to tell i'm
learning to tell time
is learning to tell time
his learning to tell time
this learning to tell time

being 1:11, almost, she couldn't
quite tell what time it was when
the earthquake hit

WHEN I READ

ROW 15—A TO F

three people asleep in row 15
uncomfortable
row for six with four persons
the man closest has shaved head
big lips long lashes
his seat C
he   sleeps with lips closed   D unshaven—
                                                        a style in the country we are leaving
            sleeps with mouth open   the woman in F
            sleeps with her head rolled over her very large belly
she appears young from some place other
arrives at the gate with four huge
plastic bags full of gifts for baby   drags the largest on the floor
                                                        grips passport and ticket between teeth
there is a fuss
who let her through the gate with
loose bags like these
            they board her anyway
            help her store gifts over heads

soon out our window Alps push from earth
                        in a morning light for snowy peaks

HUNTING DOGS

A woman had fallen into great loneliness. Since loneliness is essential to the life of a hermit, she decided to be one. She sent away even her hunting dogs, for even her dogs were company. Her dogs did not understand her calling to the hermitage so they bothered her constantly and continually barked at her gate. She refused to let them in until she ran out of food. She then accepted the dry dog food of her former dogs as nutrition enough. She enjoyed their company in the pursuit of birds, for the smallest birds swooped down to pick up dry food, one kernel at a time. She joined her dogs in eating the birds that she caught and didn't think once about bird feathers sticking out of her mouth. Eventually she tried to remember what down meant, and sit and beg and heel. After many years she became a very famous hermit and human seekers came wanting to be her followers. They did what she did, for she said nothing.

WHEN I READ

When I read the first sentence about women turning into cedars in a corner of a graveyard, I thought of the little church and graveyard in Greece where wind whistles through a cluster of cedars making an awful sound. They say it is the sound of the old women buried there. As widows they always wear black and say little directly except to the children. All day they only murmur foul phrases to everyone else at every turn. Nothing is enough, *skata* is not allowed and all their shoes look like slippers so we never hear them coming. Here, halfway from there, a freeway runs at the back of our property. My husband thinks of planting cedars along the back wall bordering the freeway and I worry. Brushing up against each other, a line of cedars can grow to be a wall. I can't have a row of women screaming that I am wrong or that I haven't done this or that. If he goes ahead with his plan, I will have to slink out in the dead of night with a hatchet to cut them down.

GRIZZLY MAN AND WERNER

There is a man who does not know the color of his own eyes. He'd rather not, he says. He has an aversion to psychology and introspection. Still he says he knows of those who keep strangling rabbits so they know they are alive. He quotes a French writer that said one should live one's life with moderation and save extremes for art. The man, who has not seen his eyes, says his wife calls him a fluffy man. Others know his films and think he is not. He says in response that it would be over his dead body that the recording of the death of the grizzly man would be available through his art. He says no one deserves to die like grizzly man died, even though he was alienated and thought everyone else crazy.

POSSESSIVE PRONOMINAL ADJECTIVE

There are two brown spots on either side of the walkway from the house to my studio.
Correction: there won't be two brown spots on either side of the walkway from the house to my studio.
Correction: there won't be two brown spots, one on either side of the walkway from the house to my studio.
Correction: there won't be two brown spots in the lawn, one on either side of the walkway from the house to my studio.
Correction: there won't be two brown spots in the lawn where the dogs lie, one on either side of the walkway from the house to my studio.
Correction: there won't be two brown spots in the lawn where the dogs lay, one on either side of the walkway from the house to my studio.
Correction: there won't be two brown spots in the lawn where the dogs lay, one on either side of the overgrown walkway from the house to my studio.
Correction: there won't be two brown spots in the lawn where the dogs lay, one on either side of the overgrown walkway from the house to our studio.
While I am in the studio making these corrections, my husband is out on the lawn fixing the sprinkler heads that one of the dogs bit off during *its* long days in the yard between the house and our studio. If I don't use *its,* someone may think that my husband has taken to biting off sprinkler heads. He's not there yet.

PROOFING TAKES UP APRIL

4
How could she leave this space between could and forgive, followed by not having a belly button? What does forgive have to do with such lack? Bellybutton, whole hole. This anomaly could truly temper a striptease. Webster, an authority on striptease, buries his hands between his thighs. There is without exception a thread between belly and all understanding. We know.

7
We have not set foot in, Brazil, lived there, period. We know the finality of—period.

8
Ta ta, she said and noted—how much better to frame every answer without a question. No one knows or cares that the width of an n has a purpose unto itself. Lead in the belly and at the center of such a thing as heavier gravity. But we would never be brave enough to accompany her to Brazil, period. Even if little birds in the distance are ws.

9
To use quotes is more than interesting and you say—in the background—call a bird in a cage a *fledgling*. And we think to address you as Mr., although you are willing to shape our nest, *n'est-ce pas*? Ours is a delicate question of twigs and thread. Mr. preens. I can get him to—Flannery's bird.

10
Regardless. Regards and irregardless. We begin with a question of birding and music of verbs. We could call one *papagalos* and in this distinct language, disregard gender—a babel-bird in the simplest case. Let us never imagine vermin with carelessness.

14 – 16
Possessing vowels has no monetary value. It's that simple. Form is answers that follow questions with answers almost always present there. It is fine to ride a scooter but not behind the backyard fence where dogs go crazy about territory and think it provocation. That strip is a small piece of land, not darkening Brazil.

19
All this for someone who stays anonymous, it seems, unless we google her. And it remains a fragment so, finally.

31
Now to medicine. Language is more precise, surprises amid lyric, even to say what is. Take for instance hypo- and hyper-. The latter is Graves and grave. Balance is difficult with upper case, not impossible, as the other is deeper by far. Admire constant sufferers. We do from far. Experience is limited to time and this is called blessing.

35
Early on we all learn to spell encyclopedia. It is brilliant to sing a spell cycle of knowledge and one small grain scratches out a circle. We foreground, not clinging to a smooth stone, but a gathering of mice.

45
If we point one finger to a sky, three fingers point back. And she photographed the red-sky delight. A woman artist paints a slew of sled dogs swirling in an eight towards her sky. Young mountains are stylized to such an extent that dogs seem noble, the driver ignored. Still, an image is hers and hallmarked, so far so good. For a woman, this is progress somehow.

50
Some know what's right; there is guide by which. Some resent it, think on their feet almost all the time. Measures are suitable in politics, so there.

51
The consistency of *towards* is a priority.

54
He jacketed a light green suede thing. He tried her on for himself and she found him unbearable.

55
Going to the playground is an idea, not done.

56
Oh, God, here is someone who knows the root of corn and wants her to know. Who is this who is so direct and speaks directly?

59–60
We go back and count words for this one. Nothing is reasonably anything. Or nothing is reasonably anything exact, least of all reasonably clean and light.

61
There is repetition, a question of dam and damnable. We study these questions in third grade—a first book in a series. We believe after years of what—it is (repeat)—it is legitimate when a word such as dam looks like what it is. We unfortunately did not photograph the photograph of the peasant on his knees before they flooded his valley. We drank ouzo on a balcony over a lake—treetops grew out of water. His coat is blowing and his hair. He can't speak of this place

any longer, never place, never land and he is black specks, kneeling. Once—his and him.

62
If we never use extra space between more and you, then are we closer than we thought? It is a time thing.

66–68, 70
What exactly we have two of. We are doubled in nostrils, hands, feet, eyes, shoulders, sides, legs, knees, breasts—nipples. That's it. He is named after his upper chest. Do—nipples protrude enough—they achieve a stance without working out. He may pull at them to each hole a donut. At least we are used to the nasty air both dogs pass. We sent art by fax? Innovative for innovation—we had never seen a smear of words, we think, until that fax.

71
Variable spacing won't do.

73
Big chances are necessary. Don't let a name slip into another, for heaven's sake. Words can slip and slide—not names. They are toyed with, that's all. Overhead projectors are donated interminably. To list the past would go on. Dot doc knows *passé* requires an accent *aigu*. There is no red squiggle. *La de da* needs correction.

82
Whew. We almost blew this. She would not accept breaks. It was breath, most likely, that was her guide.

90–94

This is called a real mess. To suppose what he wants? And why change this tone? When confessional is not acceptable, is it also witness?

103 and further

a. Poetry is bright with color. Green does not allow red, but only as afterthought.

d. A need to remember without knowing what. The familiar need in families. A chain made of hair is perfect—100 years ago.

f. Orally non-sentences do not exist. It is dialogue. No exists not in dreams.

g. A onetime adventure is hardly a pattern. A onetime adventure is a pattern.

118

We find it no longer large. There's little at large. Responsibility invades us. This end diverges, sad divergent end.

To tell in the dark which it was
To tell in the dark where it was
To tell in the dark when it was
To tell in the dark how it was
To tell in the dark why it was
To tell in the dark who it was
To tell in the dark yet it was
To tell in the dark if it was
To tell in the dark time

PARIS OCTOBER 12

that methodology delivers patience seems true
before recording   when painting is real   not lost in time
wait   dead horses are to painting as music is
no one wants to hear that   much less
create from hearing or after and fearing   for endurance
and what breaks down   fear
not even time or splendor of thought
temporal yet   lasting as splendor does
as thoughts with music   to represent holding   again
what's new   not remotely heroic   unless there is banding
together   great music as its own
while fear of a lack   lacks confidence   is obvious
avoiding the obvious is there   undoubtedly
pleasure in re-working   in patience   hmm

"Everyone is more disturbed by his least trouble than by the most signal disaster of a whole nation." (1822)

TUESDAY OCTOBER 22

loving painting and eye   yes   eye
simple mention of eyelids and eyebrow   lovely space
wait   the confounding I in sound   envisions
you'll go blind   reading in the dark
Sanctus   Ignatius would have us direct vision
sight and sensitivity to light   the more   see who cares
obsessive painting   caring about it   caring for it
carrying around painting   painting in general
like four walls   and on walls
spots in embryos   the sitting upon a stalk
the eye is hung and swivels
ever shielding eye   and framing
a seat of judgment   ocular   oracle
pink from hand to eye   twinkle twitch

"As usual my slight build abashes me." (1822)

LAST TUESDAY

surprisingly enough   other months have ides
beware the French valise
and does the god of war   of (all things)   deserve a month
then imagine   when Tuesday is 13
a bag and rhymes with   not wanting to
perhaps trash falls more equivalent   like walking right hand
left foot   the energy to take a big chance
and her and paint her   carrying disease   to be sure
like painting a painting   our Marie is ancient
she may be gone for years   haven't seen her body on walls
bronze could be a first metal mined   the whole Marie
of   anything a sublimation   ouch
asking   for the sake of dwelling   in chance
tin and copper   chancey

"I have resumed my violin." (1822)

PARIS TUESDAY APRIL 15

probably dark still night of the next day early
breathe and breath on air and whinney some gentler tone
of and feeling like waking this not out question of dreams
sounding far from whining *Matins* in horses
Saying neigh you, *Hellenides* apparently affirming
so very early and watching and watchman unforeseen
the younger watchman lives in a car
simple enough statement
only that he is young among
taking a shower of air and light slowly
do I need to know sleeping on the floor or standing
stable this google question of equines
also asses to a zebra take off those pajamas
git in here

"Today I made several good resolutions." (1823)

MONDAY JANUARY 12

things to consider　　　lilies for instance
they neither　　and you know each and every
trying to forget　　　not even the lilies whose tell-tale signs
the owned　　the tell-tale *e*
displacing money　　　with wrinkles
keeping mind　　　I'll file it here　　　a visual prompt
the virgin Mary　　　and as subject
keep in mind her skin must be　　　the betrayal　　the truth
what then makes　　　for unevenness and flab
crock and cock　　　it seems
forget yourself to be forgotten　　　in a crevice
trying it slippery　　　and wet
the better slippage　　　staving off
and this ultimate throat

"Unhappily, she carried off part of the energy that I wanted for the day's work." (1824)

SAME DAY

what the old men know   as reported
and caught napping
believing everything   you read
knitting with the wool   over
your own eyes
better a pair of mittens   than a cap
the age old question
of cause   and effect
lazy nations don't get it   I think
the comfort of pop songs leads us
letting go fitfully
it's natural   as day and night
saving sleeping for night
falling   as into sleep

"Very important." (1824)

SUNDAY JANUARY 25

why   admit it   slipping and slippage
for who knows   as for the future receding
from us as does the past before us
Where is about fucking?
as soon as we see it so   it too no longer is
you know   going over events
imagining through another   as stepping in steps
there are other ways   out of a labyrinth
as long as
there is no lid   I see there is   over
walking on heads   and intimate space
attaching a body limb by limb
while planting a memory   in someone else
this sort of re-minding

"They have their own cross to bear." (1824)

SATURDAY APRIL 10

strange and beautiful   at once
think about it—
my, my
how opposites is from   opposed
contours smooth and thin as a line
to separate night from day   is one thing
softness is thick   dimensional   actually and night
calling the edge vigorous and so   liminal
not purgatory   not sinless   not guiltless
more than so
lord   it would be a fabrication of life   really
we would be as   as they say   or said
like Warhol's edge and   someone's messy inside
said the old woman   she kisses a cow

"The pure noses. All this is what I have always been seeking." (1824)

TUESDAY APRIL 20

the pretext of a headache   who of us haven't
analgesics kick in   like motors
and what is there   about pretext   a moment too ancient
too long a stretch to ax
to be used as a pretext   an excuse to   a web before
text would be a surprise   to all perhaps a source
of validity   a skin   no—tissue
so time passes   not any longer time
in the present   at least
when the wind changes   mark time
only irregularly   only invisibly   under disguise
except for its effects   headaches and leaves fall
the angle of   a headache
leave me out of this one

"I myself, I will pass away, too. This also is a consolation." (1824)

SATURDAY MAY 15 DURING THE DAY

seamless comes to mind
a painting is not grammatical therefore not done
grammatically lesson one
and thus follows
by painting a painter is
if you listen very attentively to your doctor and it ends
there being clever in painting it should stand
zero in on pleasure and pain although preachy
may not be a word the word their word
do what's best with regard to either
that's virtue you see especially
about pleasure
for this is common to animals reason enough not
to eat meat

" . . . that what has been said has still not been said enough." (1824)

BOOKKEEPERS

The first bookkeeper didn't want to be one. Sometimes we found her walking around the office in her bare feet. The first time, she said the bottoms of her feet were sunburned. After that we didn't bring it up. What she wanted to be was a belly dancer. Once we hired her and her group for a public relations event, and it was true, she wanted to be a belly dancer.

The second bookkeeper had a very floral hand that she had developed growing up somewhere in the Middle East. For years after she left, we recognized her files and work sheets by her handwriting, and we would say, "That is her handwriting."

The third bookkeeper was young and dishonest. We checked our phone bills and found his family's out-of-state phone number listed often enough. When we called them they gave us their address without any problem. Then they got the letter accusing their son of pocketing sums of cash meant for deposit. They sent a lawyer the next day to settle up. We don't know if the son learned any lesson, but we got our money back.

The fourth bookkeeper was an American Indian. We didn't want to believe that she used the petty cash to repair her car, but she put the repair receipts right in the petty cash envelopes, so there was no question. The state employment department said we could even press charges. We felt sad about that whole history stuff, so we didn't.

We liked the fifth bookkeeper. On the boss's birthday, she and one of the other women ordered a stripper dressed as a cop, then she covered her eyes because she couldn't watch. Other than that, for five years, she just kept the books.

ON PORTO

1

water rushes a slope—down slope—even I know that; the rush to collect is a practice—gathering stones for walls and stacking them—a craft; were harvesters with their wooden rakes always immigrants; it is the owners who prune and graft a pinwheel of productive shafts—make it light and airy for both sun and rake—perfect shape—comb fruit into nets; rakes are not more than shafts with dowels and pole; the sensibility of a practice occurs in healthy states; it is a common sense; glory be to gravity; stone and still there—gone and still there—even for centuries

2

I can hear his quick decision *ethó* cut it—and *ethó*—here—*ethó* he says again; neighbor—this neighbor-man takes no prisoners; we are strangers to Porto and a town below—we barely throw anything out—nothing is too low below; this second house in a second country is full of old pots old dishes old towels—old and below; I climb hills—alight on a terrace—stir ashes and take a record specimen; I make a photo of his work; I am thieving in the neighbor's grove—mapping evidence; the formal demands of clearing slopes—keeping height from taking over—and over each year; am I tempted to be here

3

there is the first question; the questions of why; why circles of ash; not how or when (the older question) why—stripped of time—dates add nothing to my memory—only in this sense could the question be; but it's not at all—all of it—at heart; there is a fear of exclusion in answers; I've stumbled on a curiosity—not mine—someone else's carefulness and labor not mine; I tell myself that I wouldn't; wander into a neighbor grove—when and if—if I lived here year round in this blankety place—not on an opposite side of anything; at all

4

should I read them as condensation—these circles of ash; the neighbor plows up to—right up to—our contentious fence—and the ashes—not the *remember man that thou art* palm *dust* but pruned disposable olive limb; how our easement is on his mind; can we in good faith object to a mind; his *ktima* is plowed ours is not—our unplowed *ktima*—it's mathematical; if *what* meant something other than *what*—like for instance *x*—I could think this through I think; so that if *x* had happened and *x* could mean any number of things and why meant *y* in this about-time-face—I would have a conclusion; but no I have simply taken the liberty of walking his grove; how wordy; there is evidence of liberty—I carry my one time camera

5

it is embarrassing—these lopped off limbs; soldiers lose limbs; just where they begin and end—not there; the sequence of father then son makes little difference—a war is war; in my humble pie awareness—it is a fleshly appearance we avoid and face if it appears—if it is on our stupefying watch; we are light and stupid to the last; this is a new methodology; I am feeling too much (con) fusion with the trees—"O trees of life when will your winter come"—it will; yes; *Hector* don't go—the state is not worth it; not for glory less for revenge

6

I am old now as a tree; I am also productive; productive years are up to one hundred and fifty; they say; an old tree is never cut down—it is made to remember; this old one peels back its own skin—lets soft show through; it is overtly tied to late prophecies; or politics—however bizarre—a tradition; it believes in prophets until it takes a gun to its head in lieu of medication; no one can believe I'm not on medication—at my age knock on wood; at my age; to say sorry if I disappoint—the old bitch; I can't even use that word for the local stray; our black *Bella*.

7

chaos of accretions and deposits are evidence of its underworld life; water-borne washed; who can define where this specimen begins or ends; Ah—*Demeter* has damaged her stock lying with her brother; blame her (not her brother) and see; Hades delights in confusing Persephone—she is allowing his wishes to confound her—so long in his darkness; he tricked her with his red-seeded pomegranate—now evidence of her mother's barrenness and swirling winter frost; imagine—frantic Demeter's festival is there—still—in *Frosty O's* and elfin *Trix*

8

this twinning the neighbor let it happen; words are unique and cannot exist in double; doubleness; doublings; and double talk—that's what we halve; fork-tongued is a worry to some; a mother's tongue is first in mind always; in his and theirs; yet the unique already always split—part and whole; we say something; we cannot say only the truth—something and truth are parallel to this day; we say tree but this is not truth; tree is something—that's all; a mother-in-law's tongue suspended; still grows toward the sky; once—I saw photographed evidence

9

only in words are we aware; big whoop—no tree is aware of its comical slant; each tree is only responsive; awareness goes the moment it is given; look how it swoops and produces—this bottom line exists even in the grove; each winter pruning supports it; Ulysses bathed in oil—his scent—the scent of residue outside any olive press; outside my mother-in-law's island house; for instance; he reeked of oil—a press can be anywhere; no zoning—not even a hall of records; land is owned from memory—small things; rocks—a plow turns—a slash of red paint on a tree; set a boundary; I've seen stolen rocks

10

in May even the bedding is bone dry brown; plowing turns up stones; kills grasses; leaves clumps; did I say brown again; a tree is as deep and wide; a tree is as wide and high; this grove has no drip system—all is dust; every move lays a coat in the house; this house of cement—strong and misplaced—stores water; it is kept as coin in cisterns and tanks and barrels; wasps thinking they can skim die on the surface; luckily I can't always hear—all the infinitesimal life there is there; we share this place casually; we are not always on top—not that our practice is buddhistic

11

how life compensates the urge; the day is hot—this is indecent this twisting of limbs; the farmer works the tree; finds nothing mundane in the task; this field and its plowing—this hardly quotidian affair; the farmer's *ethós*—I mean language for *here*—are almost heroic; and what of this memory of what has been; let it go; it doesn't serve his promiscuous purpose—this uncompromising practice of shaping; every thing can be erased but its memory; yet in erasure there is blindness that is ultimate; outside of it; and what looks like an opening; an orifice grays and seals over—each one with its new boundary; so—it is ended

12

an unlikely gesture here—no sense of discretion; as if we know language well enough for language to triumph over language; there is grace and graciousness however deceptive; logic is in the realm of judgment—meaning in another; the grove is in full light; in the shadow of myself I see from above and at see-level; to find harmony in all this radial beauty—I circle trees—zigzag soar and swoop; there is a darkness that light presupposes; there is; I can turn into hawk—young at flight; but can I practice a hawk's eye against clear blue; that too bright for sight

13

things are stopped; things are halted; families may know nothing of what went before—in a grove trees are property—carrying a body of knowledge; hiddenness is impossible for the sake of disclosure and forgetfulness for memory; latency is our farmer's inspiration; a scion is grafted—latches onto a termination; catches on; our farmer waits; knows fully that his choice is competent; there is a feeling like swimming in a sea that has no tide or currents worth fighting; he may even fertilize although I've never seen it; families are farmed; although can't end it

14

who will not say this resembles a phallus; overpowering and vehement—a slim chance alone; we are bursting; it is bursting; the light small noises and stones distract me; I stop long enough to frame the click—enough is enough—here where I stop; now in black and white and shadow; I see—to believe I have; among visible things—glory of sun and axe; equivalents are visual and conscious; I repeat my observations as a scientist would; with repetition we form a body of knowledge; this organization of potentiality; is not lost on me; no matter—the study is not ending

15

how the outer form falls in folds is unnerving; it is more a sign of the tree's refusal to forget—scars on my chin where cells were removed; I think of heredity—there is no space for surprise; I've seen it again; a relentless repetition of cutting and healing; where is unconsciousness kept; where our dreams; so long ago that we can't remember—to open a new place—to imagine it; in his bed he dreams he is Crusoe; we are all home made; he resourceful—he always was

16

clouds are rare all summer long; soon I will use the sky to tell weather; soon I will be able; it is common here—forked sticks find source for water—to believe a diviner; to hire one and drill where he says to drill; there is little; water at a premium; locals say what water there is—is salty; bad wells; no water; bad water—to speak of; our pump never raises more than a few liters; at once; it is ours for years not enough; now it sits on the floor—for years; my father watches Friday; with pink milkshakes she minces around the room; the bed; she made it from scratch—she is (con)founded about what more to do; bad well; bad water; not well again

17

see how low they keep the trees rake ready and sunned; I am becoming a grove; (g)ods took lovers in groves; a mere setting; a lower case almighty for their gods' fears and doubts; the small sounds in the plowed ground will last forever; can anyone in the face of such small and numerous murmurs—not turn into someone else; am I tempted to be here; who said—I think where I am not—therefore I am where I do not think; not me; the road looks easy; it's not; it doesn't look; that's all—watch out for that branch and duck

18

this oldest of the lot is *dissed*; a disgusting old tree; rusted chain link leans into its garrulous trunk; they haven't fenced it—the town; they are not announcing its age how old; they would say that it's old very old—just that; few words—they would compare it to themselves; it will outlast them; it has; like a house it can't be moved but should be; misplaced—how a misplaced house; can a tree be an ancestor of man; they love this thing; it is one more—many old fishermen trailing sea things

19

we drive to Porto with a four-wheel—fly through witchy grove; can't stop; use momentum to mount the holy hill—we push us up; in winter the road turns to a minor river; I don't know which method works best—track the ruts; avoid the rocks; watch out for trees; passengers suffer; the road goes around an olive tree each and every—every time; it may still be law—it was in antiquity; I promise I will not move there; before she dies

20

patterns of shadow creep slowly over land—grove-scape—below the house; we call it homely precisely—not homey—homely; it is too close to ugly—and latent until—we will live there always—inconvenient not familiar; what means survival means; there are few signs of anything other than groves sky and sea; I sweep the house for the seventh time—wait for shadows to disappear into night; the town lights; in town there are *kafenions* but we stay here—listless in the overwhelming presence of nature; she has died still not ready

TERRIBLE/GEOGRAPHY

ZAY UND ZITA

start   no begin not far
                         slightly east on a map
at the mouth   bushes like islands
                         and south
slowly float away   a protecting head
call it warmer than twice as far across
a terrible geography   is *Bedlam*
hot   against all sky
before ocean and world ocean highway
men wear heads no caps
pin where we are   on a promenade deck

                         sail across to
the land of *Zay und Zita*
clogged with silt slowing smooth yellow sea
earth washing   at once these two oceans
no longer than from   clear to muddy brown
whole points of land   float round
a flat plate tips   to drain what of can't be
new shore of blue lines
the thinnest dresses
make way   we come to
leaving off sweaters
            in most of the world

RUG IN TURKISH

a mud dark cockatoo on this *kelim*
—a traveler's first day and
faith in god's
in the beginning 'in the isolation of the sky'
—her first division is still Monday
void without a name
—this thing, this earth is not but firmament

•

dark ballooning native pants surround a paraclete

she stirs beside the waters
(day is like wide water, without sound)

her place beside is blue in blueness

kusadasi
ephesus
izmirni out of exile
istanbul
the bosphorous

—song bird of restoration

•

further to annul division
—and water cutting east from west, the see of black and marmara

the light

—is good in their blue mosque around each shoe and ringing column
—give way to strangers, stranger
still, the silent
horns and rush of wind

•

not this dividing and indifferent blue,
she is leaving darkness on its own
it will be night on some fourth day
nor to mention a lesser light than rules it

what else

then is reversed —if evening and the morning are first day
—out of order, so

•

is it—the thought of heavens in a palace room of script
not scripture

to ask can one high priest extend his blackened limbs to sink
thus casually into darkness

why not

—herself is there beside the stirring
this ambiguous undulation

SALINE

way before breakfast
way before I usually leave for work
I call Norma she is east
this is business
I know her voice hear
its voice-mail version in
Saline Michigan over again (must be lake-coastal—
the reference to salt)
it's an either/or take or leave and don't ask

what is time
what time is
who's serving it not why but what
for further details use the full-on
navigation system
a drag of knots counting beats

press one
if you want to avoid
the long explanation
it may not apply

she is busy stringing another line
or just not there or if still (still there)
around somewhere used to almost
expecting a page
a full moon tangle

accidentally drawn tight
some quarter lapse of time
and we tie nerves   so bundled under star blood sails
                    my own voice crackles

OLD GROVE

there is a can't conceive
in olive groves
pruned by slashing
and lashing
star fish limbs   appended there in air
old groves
pile up slag and lump and
bend to still
give

out
          cold stone fruit

MATOULA'S

I sip fish soup in
"Matoula's old Restaurant"

an eye of a fish head flavors and stares
at us who float above
why it's disheveled
Yannis Ritsos never leaving his *Monemvasia* climbs
out his spring cold bed
past well-used toys of local *pedi* interred nearby
local lucite headboards preserve beribboned bears red trucks
to oddly outlast whirling women
who cherished them
his plot of land
their *ktima* measure

Yannis
his face on painted stones still useless still his work
slips up a fortress hill thin balconies for
this a terrace so well understanding what is slope

with strange surprise of sputtering holes
small white lights on limbs string all our nights together

AT NO EASE

this infestation shepherd out to lunch a closer time
shining eyes dark round each stinking nest and lock them in
live off the contents there's a house there's a cave
in contempt of speaking
in Didyma means twin

each drawer and crevice closing in and locking up
winter's cold enclosure

unwelcome
after three days a fish stinks
in in Didyma meaning
in a twin circle of eyes comes first in earth's hollow
O himself O journey signing O and no man and men held in
a howl and no playing
tunnel wide on not on this side wide an other
underside no man and men blinding
take a stake and bleating host

pink pellets pliers our
resource O eye of our underbelly
cling breathing in and holding breaths
for too long time

AFTER JACK PASSING

these are the poems after Jack's passing
hill and gully rider
hill and
gully
these are the ones no one sows
under hill the real skinny *gully*
if to know some thin only
again 'twas July 02 he died

jeepers creepers where'd he get those scars
but the story when and if
it's not joe ours
it is just too thin
the girl's not Jane or Jill or home
in the end
I can't even answer even blubbering
imbibering
An Irish *taint* it
hiding a bottle as a divorce in a stereo oh oh

like a skeleton in the closet
'n on our front door
yearly the day of dead victuals
draping *dem* bones *so's*
the battle for potatoes
a soup with
no cream that drives men and more so
to the big really scary
trip peregrinations

so back to Jack
his passing that's a fact   I'm sorry for
jack   when whatever's
the opposite of eyelids sag
you can't help but feel sorry
for the days Jack had
                               so what's the story
the singe no the sear

                               of fire
                               dimple *'n* dappled
                               skin shadow skin
and how do you get left with
only three fingers by the by

keeping it all to *'emselves*
the fire   *them's* fighters
where's a finger go in fire
letting not knowing sink in
where's the finger
a body in loam sinks and mud
                               and muddy war
                               what
pride of Jack
and World Old War II

MILK

after a bath in milk   she washes
hair   braids it
toss a cat's tail
          no reason not to take herself
          her bruises away

the cat traffic diminishes   and
the mother of the bride
collects one more stray   tapes
          a message for the milkman
do not feed the cats   they will
                                        think

                                        they are home

SCAT BLUES

I've trad upon a patch, I'm veared a shall go scat —1867 Rock

right is like a mitre—it sprawls
          over supper
it sprawls over ridges of a bowl
it sprawls under cushions
          and treads an ass there
its blue—your path
          is chiseled
to the bottoms of your feet
                    asphalt under wheels
there are bruises of your skin
          on the coolness of the mirror
and on the ridges of a bowl

TABLEAUX VIVANT

a representation of
the action at
some stage in a play
created by the actors
suddenly holding
their positions or 'freezing'
especially at a moment critical
to the plot or at the end
of a scene or act.
also as a stage direction.

DIRECTION 1

a flower comes felled   after (me)
a bridge passes broken over (us)
a baker looks solitary on as obsession
is reborn blind   out(side)
a fake pine   branches fold trimmed and   (all)
old men shimmer against themselves
take care   stumble transient almost
an eagle grows in mid-air a(way) from the canopy
time seems short for sure   (there's a beach)
(I) hear barren inside
when an apple
blushes in candy pink
light is early and water
goes soft

DIRECTION 2

others fly by this thin dry wall
years asleep wonder at sand   while birds
dread singing   still (yours)
her neck slips cold in the shade
(and) sundown passes torch-lit   on
a bicycle as rush reels the light (shimmer) shiver
at last runs streaked with rain   out of range
somebody dies briefly   sometimes is (tomorrow)
an afterthought mistakes point glorious   (sorry for this)
still rain turns away rain-wet malevolence
and darkness leads back   towards (belongs)
to walls (of) clear neon now
the sky goes and seeps small bonfires
(I'm) afraid a sports car dips   the red (shimmy)

DIRECTION 3

tales bleed inside woman
memory leading to clear then (a)round
snow takes no time at all into unresisting (snow)
it throws concerns for all (future) now
wickedness slams trashcans so hard that
water is crying as down to the river (as)
faraway I hear dust the stippler is waiting
night is confused as daring (down)
a tune mutes as it speaks paper-thin
(and) a window leans as big as reason (why)
fabric loses shafts of laughter every (day)
a hill dying on the ground plays a strident sound
a father is still (blue) Ireland green
a pillow placed bunched up (under)

DIRECTION 4

shadows die shifting   red hair (flames)
a corner whispers to creep round to night
merely air   sways knowing a refrain
the wind plays (fair) luck as
a woman walks unseen blocking views   (blocking)
she thinks of remarking neither black nor lace
a long dinner closes at the end (by) slipping (away)
the moment lives for a moment all of a summer
a wheel slows down rapt by a (circle) fittingly
sun-seeking without thought   wide out(side)
every star a long yet still alive
hail where are you   never-ending like some picture of
waters spreading something to (do)   little maniacs writhe
(wet) and tender

DIRECTION 5

surrender a bad start   (to)
notes why wake up anymore
but as I walk   (I am) no longer
there could there (ever) be such a place
she listens with a glance a settling in
light that touches earth shakes
the waiting for (seeing) him again
the birds go up   winged   alone
sit in   (all stands)   a word for trees
fast fading also faster
where'd the sun
the waves are steep waves
now that worries her   the furniture
from the corner closest (to) dream (from)

DIRECTION 6

have mercy   the humming of
children shows up   go smile (until)
it stops   this the sound
of fear nothing
so unworthy of your live the life (of)
a monk on the outskirts and all
be like that   and still survive
summer sinking   left to say
accept (of course) in speaking
only fair mercy   I keep many colors
but just how heroic my heroes (are)
step on a crack to wake up this un easy
satisfaction
and all that decreasing   expanse

DIRECTION 7

as a waterfall follows drowning in
the street (left) behind
music careful and multiple like   the opposite of (felt) is
lovely   and works so impossible to intrigue (her)
a man knows a flickering object   a zephyr
holds whiteness all around in simple hums
of a panel of   wonder at the trivial in   (the) flesh
off glad hands high honey
she whips   with strings as a red coming of age (and)
any object has no synonym   to insure
become   an abundance of some inflation
though a starveling   ranges (over all)
and hovers so close
for reasons kept stippled   then never (left)

DIRECTION 8

a border grants twisting access to a river (over)
plains end in   I'm told   the skies (an)
odd   returning with all the lettering
a raven kind-of looks rarely in here   in (this)
space that awaits our ordered waiting
this side departs doing a brisk return (so)
place gets a high volume of what-to-do-now
and walls hear ranging within each other
come back   for (longing)
at the (end) passing over   I am still here
a noise on a buzz towards the edge
giants stretching until now near naked
a small vowel picks up the sounds of birds in wind
my kite flies   get up again (to) (kick)   my heart

CAVAFY

My husband's friend, the one whose house we stay in on the island, says that the old neighbor woman next door is the only woman who takes care of him, who isn't looking for his wallet. No sooner are we through her balcony door than she is offering a small coffee and a homemade sweet on a spoon, a bitter one like an exotic jam. Her cookies are especially healthy. They are made with olive oil only, no butter or eggs although she keeps chickens in the yard that lay plenty of eggs. For our friend she'll bring out a blood pressure cuff to take a reading. He expects to be healthy on the island. He gets disappointed when he walks the mile and a half from the harbor to his house and his blood pressure rises. My husband tries to tell him that he should take his blood pressure when he has been at rest and not after a brisk walk. At night after a meal of local fish and tomato salad our friend reads Cavafy in Greek to us on the balcony of his island house. It sounds like good poetry and although I don't know what he is saying, it seems like a very good reading.

PIECES

On the island the neighbor woman and her husband are broad bodied with enormous worker hands. They have a pureness, not a clean kind of pure, but one that comes from being clear like glass is clear. The husband's face and especially his long large nose are a ruddy red. He fishes for squid and octopus and other local fish many times a week and never protects himself from the sun. He also has goats that he allows to run free day or night. They come back to him when they are ready to be milked. He makes goat cheese that he gives to the neighbors. One evening he brought over a few birds, something quail-like that his wife had prepared for our friend's dinner table. We had to be careful not to bite down on the shot pieces that were embedded in their bodies. They were tasty and we left the shot pieces and tiny bones on our plates. On the island we always talk about fishing and where to find fish. We feel we are living real life and always sleep restfully in our friend's island house. In the morning we step on the stone floor and walk to the window to open the blue shutters, never knowing what to expect from the weather. If the eucalyptus trees are not blowing and the sea looks calm it does not mean that the hydrofoils to the mainland are operating. The sea could be dangerous out in the open and we wouldn't know it. The last time we were leaving the island, there was an earthquake that was only felt with any force right above where the plates had shifted because its center was thirty to forty miles below the sea.

ORTHODOXY

The neighbor's wife suggests we visit a nuns' monastery on the other side of the island. She is a believer in orthodoxy as is our friend who is becoming more and more spiritual as he grows older. We decide to visit the monastery and so take a boat to the other side. There are more than three hundred stairs to the top. At the top before entering the church the women in our party take sack skirts off hooks near the bells to wear over their shorts out of respect. The nuns ask the women if they are orthodox. They lie and say yes. The men had warned the women that the nuns would not accept anyone who was not orthodox. Then they offer lunch for a small donation in a dining room that is reserved for special visitors to the monastery complex. The dining room is full of embroidered cloths, samplers and pillows with crosses and unknown texts. Photographs of severe spiritual directors decorate the walls. We eat a simple meal and do not say too much in order not to give away the lie. The men and the nuns share one language and the women and the nuns share another. The nuns are capable in both languages, but no one knows if they think the women share a language with the men. On the way down we pick greens for salad and rest in the shade of overhanging rocks. Before we leave the two nuns agree to let us take a photograph of them. They are laughing in the photograph and the lilies from their garden with their trumpeting faces toward the sun are in the background.

BRATSERA

They converted a sponge factory to a romantic island hotel. The woman who owns it inherited it from her family. Each room has a balcony, some overlook a courtyard and some a winding stone road in the center of the island's only town. All the rooms are painted with a warm burnt umber watercolor wash. Someone applied it with a sponge and brush and left lots of streaks and texture. Their hand and rhythms are everywhere. The rooms have double beds with mosquito nets draped from the ceiling. Guests leave the balcony doors open without fear of bites. Some think that the owner made some mistakes—she devotes too much space to the bathrooms. They are almost as large as the bedrooms. And then she hires young people, who look like models to staff the front desk. They know nothing about service or find service below them. They do each speak three or four languages and use them in discourses with the tourists. A pool surrounded by an arcade of thin white columns is long and narrow and dramatically lit within the hotel's outer walls. The hotel is called Bratsera, the name of a vessel where the sponge workers rest after their harvest on the sea floor. A dry well with a wooden bucket stands near the entrance. The water from that well was once used to clean the living matter from sponges. Sponge diving used to be the island's main occupation. It no longer is. Still sponges are sold everywhere and few know they are using what is a skeleton to absorb fluids or rub off dry skin.

ORACLE

A group of tourists visited a sacred place where once there was an oracle. Not having had any experience with oracles, they enjoyed it as much as they could. The night before they were to leave the hotel and the area, they went down to a seaside restaurant for dinner. There they met a very old man who was a fisherman by day. His clothes were a grey green including his hat and jacket. His clothes were old like he was. When the dance for old men started, he danced with his coat over one shoulder, swinging his free arm and snapping his fingers like he was young and sharply dressed. The next day the manager of the hotel chased after the tourist bus on his motorbike as they drove away from the site of the ancient oracle. He would not allow the bus to continue until each person who had left with a white terrycloth robe from their room opened their suitcase and returned it. After they turned over the robes, they left in shame and no one said a word.

is learning to tell me

TRAP

At the end of their vacation and before they left for home, a couple purchased a mousetrap. They shopped around to find something their friend would like—an imported device that was artful while designed for catching mice. Some mousetraps were more like folk art than mousetraps. Some looked flimsy and obviously handmade. In the store where they found their purchase, they asked the lady to give them a demonstration. She climbed right in to show them how well it worked although it was handmade. They thought about purchasing the trap with the sales lady inside, but decided against it, since their friend had been having problems with his wife and he would not have appreciated an already occupied mousetrap. To their surprise the sales lady refused to climb out and held the door firmly closed. She had dreamed of immigrating to another country, especially to theirs. They on the other hand thought, "Nothing stays where it belongs," revealing their point of view. Then again they thought, "Her intention to break with her homeland is almost heroic." First came their vacation, then excitement over a purchase, then distraction again as they watched her extract herself from the mechanical device. Finally they were not sure what they really felt.

IN TOW

Now I'm being towed. The driver's on the phone telling his girlfriend that he's in tow and that he'll call her back later. He is teasing her about having something with him. He's said it twice. Would you believe I have it here with me? He says that to her and then he tells her where it is, wherever she is. Then he says again he's in tow and he'll call her back later. We settle back and he asks me if I'm ready for more rain. He's easy to talk to and he says he loves the rain. He says it two more times and I'm wondering what more he knows about rain than I know. He says that it's not because there are more tows when it rains. That is what I asked him. I say he must be from somewhere else and he says he's from here. I want to know if he's ever lived somewhere else and he says he has. He lived for four years in Reno and then he came back. I ask him if he's going to watch the big game tomorrow or is he going to work. He will work and he knows nothing at all about batting a football. And he adds—really. I wonder what he was teasing his girlfriend about, what he didn't have with him. He says he liked living in Reno. I ask for how long? He says—four years and then he came back. I say I've never been there, but that I know there are mountains in Reno. I tell him that I tried to go there once, but the kids got chicken pox so we had to cancel. He says that one day it went from one hundred degrees to twenty-five degrees in five minutes. The navigation system is telling him to exit the freeway at the next exit. Then the woman's voice is telling him to turn left off the exit. I say that I grew up on the east coast and I am used to rain. I say something about having old cars so that we get towed a lot and that once it was raining really hard and the same car was being towed to the same repair guy. And the driver was really scared or I was, but we didn't slow down. Now he is pulling in to the service place. He takes the car down and out from all the ropes and chains attaching it to the truck. He's already let me know that the alternator is busted. There was a tiny shock he said when he tried to jump it. He doesn't want to see my auto service card when I ask him again. Then he is flying out of the yard and waving and telling me, drive carefully now.

COW

There is a theory that restoring ancient artifacts is an intrusion in the natural life cycle of those artifacts. Of course when looking at the promiscuous lifestyle of the gods, there is the question of what is natural. Look at what happened to king Minos's wife, *Pasiphae*. She had a hollow wooden cow made by the man who carved dolls for her family. Since the king had withheld the best bull from yearly sacrifice to the underworld god, his wife, *Pasiphae*, was cursed with a monstrous lust for a white bull. She lured the bull to the hindquarters of the wooden cow into which she had climbed. It was not a pretty sight, but thus the seed that sired the *minotaur* was deposited. Embarrassed at what his stinginess had gotten her into, the king hid *Pasiphae* and her monstrous offspring in the center of a maze. Furthermore, not willing to abandon his wife, he named the thing a combination of his own name and the word for bull. The carver of the wooden cow was a jack of all trades, and father of the man who would fly too close to the sun. All this is part of eternity and time. Restoration and all related hubris is a feeble attempt at eternity.

SWIMMINGLY WITH HER

she is playful
she plays at beaches   *knees*

          what monster bull is white   *around her*
          girls string   *green*
          take the girls then with you   *swim feel safe*
          take girls to study lesson learned

she gazes all
he grazes all as white   *around*

          all this nonsense talk   *dancing drops*
          feel her long
          his massive back
          friends and petting   *touches*

what horned   *she does*   *takes*
across the sea to this   *his shore*

SHE'S IN SEVENS

what sudden cunning   *white bull*
                                         takes Evropi south   *again in sea smitten*
           she grabs on
           face nuzzles garlands   *left trailing*
                                         by her friends
her clothes then whip billow
           so babies ride beside
                                         on dolphins
                                         consoled a show-off on the seas
                                               to Crete

           naively she consorts
                                         under simply cypress when

she   *gifted from her consort with a*
                                           dog called Laelaps weapon for the hunt
                                           bronze man of little use beyond his sounding
self
                                           form living on in sky
                                                     constantly
                                         without her now

1:11, ALMOST

MISCALCULATIONS: A GUIDE

I.
I
am

going

to get to
the bottom\
to the underside.

~~~~~~

II.
Whose fault
it was and

anyway.
From the p o v
of writer, no observer, too distant

or a father—
it was the boyfriend.

~~~~~~

III.
This is too early in
A project to get to

my God, a boyfriend.
I'm sorry. It throws
everything

off.
Who I am doesn't matter.
I am the least invested

in the construction. It is
after all a project.
For better or for worse

it does not include everyone
and least of all
strangers who are not invested at all.

~~~~~~

IV.

Despite everything, in the end, at the final bell, when all is said and done, Et cetera. "The hall itself was strewn . . . with trunks, imperials, and . . . the hundred *etceteras* of traveling baggage."
I have to be honest. I can fall for
too.

~~~~~~

V.

So, yes, so,
he is ravishing

in his own way. Tall lanky musically
inclined.

You see.
I too am enamored, unarmored
of him. Strangers are

called xenia in Greek. I am
most transparent. Nothing hidden

at this moment.

~~~~~~

VI.

First report
they are never on time.
Jet-lag, no excuse.

A strange *arbeiter* has no
day of his own. Guest worker translates
all over Europe.

They are there. I am here. I am home. They
at the project site.

~~~~~~

VII.

The *kafenions* are full of men
as usual.
My favorite serves cappuccino
delicious in ceramic.

They would have breakfast there if time allowed.
They are late
as usual.

I am resting my laptop on ceramic tile.
One from Mexico
to absorb the heat.

r and *t* are right next to each other.

It wrote heart at once. Unasked for.

~~~~~~

VIII.

They are not doing well.

The boyfriend and daughter.
Strangers are supposed to be loved.
Xenia also means guest. Do unto.

Host, guest, stranger
"akin to L. *hostis*, stranger, enemy..."
~~~~~~

So not, kin.

"What good did an *outsider* ever get by meddling in a love affair?"

~~~~~~

IX.

What gods have had troubles with their daughters?
It is ongoing it seems.
Fine question, that.

I am deep within my phone conversations.
Trying not to be
inflammatory.
Taking a husband's side.
Or not.

~~~~~~

X.

All the Xenia Hotels are
a cover.
They hate strangers. I've
felt it on the plains. In the town.

It is all over town, any small town.
The stranger is neither host nor guest.
He's a boyfriend, farther outside

than I am.

Why did you come here they ask me, no
him.

He has a girlfriend. His name would be
Vassilis in Greek. It doesn't
help him.

~~~~~~

XI.
The tone of this is her tone. I don't mean
my daughter.
Give credit where it's due. He was along.

For the trip. For the job. At the job site.
Building a building. He's educated enough.
He thinks. He is. He has plans. He's not the
contractor.

A husband is a husband.

~~~~~~

XII.
They shouldn't be touching each other in
front of a father.

And is this poetry or tragedy?

~~~~~~
~~~~~~

XIII.

No touching. No nakedness.
There is propriety. Especially,

right in this little town. There is go sip.
There is drinking it in. There is watch your
back. There are two streets for strolling.

The same faces. Each day and night.
Watch your step
in either street. Eat here, eat there.

I'm talking about the basest.
Like mean-spirit.
We find dogs and save them.

There is clearly a reason.

~~~~~~

XIV.

" . . . from some obscure motive of propriety . . . "
Etymology? F. property.

My husband's second language is French.
Enough said.

~~~~~~

XV.

Boyfriend is the consummate
other.

All "others" are *kakos*. By definition as in *kakistos*.
The worst who rule and aristocrats
are best.

A lesson here. The patrician class.
Ou la la. Yes, from the root, father.
L. and literally, the fathers.

If it weren't whole cloth
I could weep now.

~~~~~~

XVI.

A boy who is a friend.
A girl who is a friend.
Likewise.

A boy who is a fiend.
A boyfriend.

The details of the project.
The noble directions. The paper
plans.
~~~~~~

Who followed what and whose
plans?

~~~~~~

XVII.

The consequence of dis—
agreement surfaces in the least likely
location. That of the building is

based on a theory of fortress.
A view to the sea and a national forest
designated behind.

Caution. Specific wording for
the forest is few straggling pines.
Am I going too fast?

~~~~~~

XVIII.

No one knows for certain.
How it happened. Measure
twice.

The window's height is wrong.
A house with a view, a window with none.
When is an eye misplaced?

~~~~~~
~~~~~~

xix.

His chair is straight, straight back.
His comfort.
How to make something comfortable…
to assure comfort.

His angle, mine.
To recline. A wife is.
That it bothers me at all.
That I am responsible.

~~~~~~

xx.

Parts of a drawing.
That there are.
This now called womanly.
If slightly diminished, what then?

Drawing by erasure. One that crumbles or
picks up ink to build up
form.
Our remains. What
working in the negative means.
I think of unwritten.

~~~~~~

XXI.

I poke for words.
He shoos them away.
Light plays on the view
partially blocked by a wild olive tree.

The one that he saved,
now whipped by the wind

GENTLE PANTRY

in
sense   a grain if true as such
homemade granola   unmade
                        remade
                        red birds use a bath in rain
                        in moisture made without hesitation

not to pop into
        to reappear as not the following day
        trimmings if not taste then the

applesauce of new
a new sense   none sense   new mmm   aah mmm
non and obviously or
sticking   move on for quite awhile
depend on
the way we do anything   new
win L   winning L   double U   ELLE
        staying free in the afternoons   for call ins
        playing with L and U across here
a recipe in chemistry for something other is united
        being careful always to   speaking from elsewhere
our joy that day over
when all is aid to double the effort effect
        to re-ignite
informal betweening listen in raindrops
        we are what's included in U
        3 5 I is all we ate and eating zero too

calling less obvious than mixing up
writing in   like 3 legged dogs or milk in a slanted light
                                   of pity and so revered
a side show of dogs
                                   in storage in cans for a kitchen garden
                                   the part about bananas
                                   a pantry at least
                                   a couple of ideas
double in fact
like folding over
and so it's wrapped

ATLANTIC

The woman glides with backstrokes along the shore. An orange-striped umbrella is in sight over her right shoulder. She moves north, her feet flapping. Her face is well out of the water as she funnels. She wears a white rubber bathing cap strapped under chin. She is most alone as she swims like this open to sky

nothing compares
to floating   I would float   bob south
same shoulder   long legs daddy
beach is long stretches
the choice   so dramatic
so rarely in pacific   waters
salt sticky head   heading hair circles
and not really slick
in spring   just so happens
flowers are   in bloom and she
has a little swim

1:11, ALMOST

The question is, does

an earthquake smell ?
When the time comes it
is essential to turn

to another side. An ice
pack where bones pinch
and save what's

left to feel alright

in this lately time.

ALONG WITH WHAT I'VE LEARNED

if there is a sucking ma in mathematics
close to moon and mouth—another
other m that measures time
they've landed on—
a world that's made of wood—
a root of true is tree—it stands
there (here) all by itself
when in kindness
what reaching—
the reach of light of a tree

JOURNAL OF THINGS I HAVE LEARNED

|01|

I am not as sensitive as I thought—I've found
simple power in

my words have life outside me
The poem is at some point out and between

I wear a snowsuit when I'm outside—in winter
all outside was white

I am outside of darkness in me
Others see it—not outside

Normally in darkness
snow freezes

|02|

I don't cry and I didn't
hate him—I should not have been so cool

he suggests I see
a therapist or something so I get

the story right—I like our stories
to disagree amicably—I live with it

To bring two lines in the same
place is overlaying

Who lays on what and what after all
is that position named?

|03|

It happens every time—time's advantage
Long distance we're in love but

a fish in three days—you know
he says it like he cares one iota—

loaves and mix-ups—for that matter—fishing
I learned to fish, once

earthworm sorry
for the hook-it pain—still

I use a pitchfork well to
unearth from dark—that pinkness

|04|

Still pre-occupied with mother
we find a floor—wide wooden planks in sleep

laid down in—it's a grocery store—even in
a story dream thinking how we

feed—form potato baskets—
crackle carrots turnips—veggies snap

in a night time grown and how woody
they will taste when we cook these

earthy matters—long spindly hairs emboss
the dirt—tubes suck moisture out

|05|

A floor plan runs around—the spiral has
no need of string to how or where

Beware—I check the time because my son
a toddler calls—at 4 am I tell him

don't you worry—I'll be home—to wait
and not be jealous—we women taking off

a ride of dreaming day
and child-care just as seamless with

walk and girdle-gossip to shake out bodies
slip deep into each—our step

|06|

Parts are under construction—women
using tape measures to calculate

the length of stairs—forms built of wood
mold cement—have an inside and outside twice measure

Nothing is too much construction
Still homes on edges are modest—women

leave plates—stacked in white drainers
They have no patterns

There is always a wall missing—is
a doll house with one whole side—gone

|07|

Consequently
what happens when seas warm I ask

how organisms
thriving without oxygen eat to emit

a smell of rotten eggs
how clouds of CO_2 first put past this simply

lid on our globe as
volcanoes cluster if enough

and spew—
how seas burp

|08|
I love brown bears who in
habit a cold rain north forest

a wood full of wander
ancient bear trails—their slim aperture winds

a short distance—I write with lumber
as bear mother cubs end in air

and love men who weep their diminish
meant and wonder at those who

fertilize a forest in fish and dream of
still rich buried eggs there

|09|
They have a way of getting under
skin—these fleshly openings

winter lisping and scarcely felt in
night a cool glass grasped and moist

so tinkling does a same small thing—lean line
a yellow back about an into wind so

no worry—it's guaranteed to
blow against this leaning with no water

to swim on air to have to
to learn to swim like this

AFTER *THE BOUNDARY OF BLUR**

I've had my coffee
I've organized my handbag
I've opened my book
I've read the first paragraph of a middle chapter
I've noted all the laptops in the waiting area
I've watched a toddler push her stroller
I've checked my boarding pass
I've stood in line
I've put on a jacket in the terminal cold
I've boarded a small commuter jet
I've chatted from the first seat, first row with a steward
I've overheard a pilot talking with a mechanic
I've heard him say maintenance glitch
I've resigned myself to missing a connection
I've seen them fiddle with buttons and knobs
I've watched the back of legs of a mechanic who wears shorts
I've heard a toddler crying
I've stayed calm myself
I've overheard a mechanic say it was never written up
I've put myself in his shoes
I've hovered attentively in a high-pitched whir
I've suspended my attention as evenly as I could

*Nick Piombino, author of *The Boundary of Blur*

ABOUT THE AUTHOR

Barbara Maloutas is the author of *In a Combination of Practices* (New Issues, 2004) and *Practices* (New Michigan Press/*Diagram*, 2003). Her work has appeared in journals including *Aufgabe, FreeVerse, Segue, Tarpaulin Sky, Good Foot, New Review of Literature, bird dog, dusie,* and *Greatcoat*. Her work is anthologized in *Intersections: Innovative Poets of Southern California* (Green Integer, 2005) and online in the 5th Anniversary Issue of *Segue* (Miami University–Middletown, 2006). In 2007 *Beard of Bees* (Chicago) published an online chapbook, *Coffee Hazilly*; *Segue* published a series of poems and an essay on writing them; and *Pronominal Pleasures* was one of four finalists with Rose Metal Press. She teaches book structures and book arts at Otis College of Art and Design in Los Angeles.

Ahsahta Press

Sawtooth Poetry Prize Series

2002: Aaron McCollough, *Welkin* (Brenda Hillman, judge)
2003: Graham Foust, *Leave the Room to Itself* (Joe Wenderoth, judge)
2004: Noah Eli Gordon, *The Area of Sound Called the Subtone* (Claudia Rankine, judge)
2005: Karla Kelsey, *Knowledge, Forms, The Aviary* (Carolyn Forché, judge)
2006: Paige Ackerson-Kiely, *In No One's Land* (D. A. Powell, judge)
2007: Rusty Morrison, *the true keeps calm biding its story* (Peter Gizzi, judge)
2008: Barbara Maloutas, *the whole Marie* (C. D. Wright, judge)

New Series

1. Lance Phillips, *Corpus Socius*
2. Heather Sellers, *Drinking Girls and Their Dresses*
3. Lisa Fishman, *Dear, Read*
4. Peggy Hamilton, *Forbidden City*
5. Dan Beachy-Quick, *Spell*
6. Liz Waldner, *Saving the Appearances*
7. Charles O. Hartman, *Island*
8. Lance Phillips, *Cur aliquid vidi*
9. Sandra Miller, *oriflamme.*
10. Brigitte Byrd, *Fence Above the Sea*
11. Ethan Paquin, *The Violence*
12. Ed Allen, *67 Mixed Messages*
13. Brian Henry, *Quarantine*
14. Kate Greenstreet, *case sensitive*
15. Aaron McCollough, *Little Ease*
16. Susan Tichy, *Bone Pagoda*
17. Susan Briante, *Pioneers in the Study of Motion*
18. Lisa Fishman, *The Happiness Experiment*
19. Heidi Lynn Staples, *Dog Girl*
20. David Mutschlecner, *Esse*
21. Kristi Maxwell, *Realm Sixty-four*
22. G. E. Patterson, *To and From*
23. Chris Vitiello, *Irresponsibility*
24. Stephanie Strickland, *Zone : Zero*
25. Charles O. Hartman, *New and Selected Poems*
26. Kathleen Jesme, *The Plum-Stone Game*

Ahsahta Press

Modern and Contemporary Poetry of the American West

Sandra Alcosser, *A Fish to Feed All Hunger*
David Axelrod, *Jerusalem of Grass*
David Baker, *Laws of the Land*
Dick Barnes, *Few and Far Between*
Conger Beasley, Jr., *Over DeSoto's Bones*
Linda Bierds, *Flights of the Harvest-Mare*
Richard Blessing, *Winter Constellations*
Boyer, Burmaster, and Trusky, eds., *The Ahsahta Anthology*
Peggy Pond Church, *New and Selected Poems*
Katharine Coles, *The One Right Touch*
Wyn Cooper, *The Country of Here Below*
Craig Cotter, *Chopstix Numbers*
Judson Crews, *The Clock of Moss*
H. L. Davis, *Selected Poems*
Susan Strayer Deal, *The Dark is a Door*
Susan Strayer Deal, *No Moving Parts*
Linda Dyer, *Fictional Teeth*
Gretel Ehrlich, *To Touch the Water*
Gary Esarey, *How Crows Talk and Willows Walk*
Julie Fay, *Portraits of Women*
Thomas Hornsby Ferril, *Anvil of Roses*
Thomas Hornsby Ferril, *Westering*
Hildegarde Flanner, *The Hearkening Eye*
Charley John Greasybear, *Songs*
Corrinne Hales, *Underground*
Hazel Hall, *Selected Poems*
Nan Hannon, *Sky River*
Gwendolen Haste, *Selected Poems*
Kevin Hearle, *Each Thing We Know Is Changed Because We Know It And Other Poems*
Sonya Hess, *Kingdom of Lost Waters*
Cynthia Hogue, *The Woman in Red*
Robert Krieger, *Headlands, Rising*
Elio Emiliano Ligi, *Disturbances*
Haniel Long, *My Seasons*
Ken McCullough, *Sycamore•Oriole*
Norman MacLeod, *Selected Poems*
Barbara Meyn, *The Abalone Heart*
David Mutschlecner, *Esse*
Dixie Partridge, *Deer in the Haystacks*
Gerrye Payne, *The Year-God*
George Perreault, *Curved Like an Eye*
Howard W. Robertson, *to the fierce guard in the Assyrian Saloon*
Leo Romero, *Agua Negra*
Leo Romero, *Going Home Away Indian*
Miriam Sagan, *The Widow's Coat*
Philip St. Clair, *At the Tent of Heaven*
Philip St. Clair, *Little-Dog-of-Iron*
Donald Schenker, *Up Here*
Gary Short, *Theory of Twilight*
D. J. Smith, *Prayers for the Dead Ventriloquist*
Richard Speakes, *Hannah's Travel*
Genevieve Taggard, *To the Natural World*
Tom Trusky, ed., *Women Poets of the West*
Marnie Walsh, *A Taste of the Knife*
Bill Witherup, *Men at Work*
Carolyne Wright, *Stealing the Children*

This book is set in Apollo MT type with Futura titles
by Ahsahta Press at Boise State University
and manufactured according to the Green Press Initiative
by Thomson-Shore, Inc.
Cover design by Quemadura.
Book design by Janet Holmes.

Ahsahta Press
2009